Federico Lepri

How To Plan A Journey On A Cargo Ship

Sail now and have the adventure of your life

First published 2015

Reprinted with corrections November 2016

ISBN 978-0-9932816-5-5

Original title: Come viaggiare su una nave cargo - vivi adesso l'avventura che cambierà per sempre la tua vita

Translated by Valentina Rossini & Gabriel W. Rowland

Edited by Brian Cross

Cover image by tatlin.net

Printed by CreateSpace

"So many people live within unhappy circumstances and yet will not take the initiative to change their situation because they are conditioned to a life of security, conformity, and conservatism, all of which may appear to give one peace of mind, but in reality nothing is more dangerous to the adventurous spirit within a man than a secure future. The very basic core of a man's living spirit is his passion for adventure. The joy of life comes from our encounters with new experiences, and hence there is no greater joy than to have an endlessly changing horizon, for each day to have a new and different sun."

Jon Krakauer

From *Into the wild*

Introduction

This book was created to help you fulfil one dream: to travel on a cargo ship. On these types of ships, there are no casinos, dancing-girls or music entertainers. There is only one restaurant and the wine list is short. If you need diversions like these to enjoy yourself, then this experience isn't for you. Shut the book now, go and book a cruise. If, instead you've been carrying inside yourself for a long time the dream to travel by sea and forge a different kind of passage away from the mundane tourist trail…if you have in you the desire for genuine adventure and escape…this is your ticket. In the next pages you will feel like you are entering what is off-limits for the majority of people.

But hold on to your excitement for just a moment while we cast a weather eye on the logistics. Booking a place on a cargo ship is very complicated. Travel agencies are not very interested in this type of trip because the profits are low. The shipping companies that provide onboard cabins for externals are reluctant to publicise. Therefore, you will have to turn to specialised representatives who provide these services. And you'll have to take care of all the booking details yourself: you will have to decide the route, prepare all the documents for embarkation, and much more. I know because I've done it.

This is how the idea to write a book about travelling on cargo ships came to my mind; a book that will explain how to organise your trip on one of these ships, step-by-step.

When I decided to make a trip on a cargo ship, I immediately started reading what other authors had written on the subject so I could gather information on how to plan my journey. However, all the books I read were mere travel diaries describing the author's life on board: what they did during the day, what they ate and so on. Information on how they managed to get on board? None. Besides, they ruined my surprise!

Don't worry, this is not a diary of my journey. This book explains how to plan your trip, and only describes life on board using the minimum words necessary.

I've been living and travelling around the world for more than ten years and crossed the Atlantic from Europe to South America as a passenger on a cargo ship. It was a journey from bygone times, in which I left behind the stress of daily life. The luxury of a cargo ship, compared to normal cruise ships, is its quiet slowness. The day passes without time schedules or programs: time is irrelevant, you manage it on your own.

Adventurous soul? A break from daily routine? Looking to meet new people? These are good reasons to make such a trip, although they may seem a bit banal. From my own travels around the world, I have learned that living in unknown and unfamiliar environments strips away one's safety blanket that modern society provides.

Thanks to my own experience and mistakes, I have been able to define some simple steps, thus enabling you to travel on a cargo ship even if you don't have any money put aside and are lacking knowledge of where to start gathering information and the necessary documents.

These are all procedures that I have followed to do my bookings. It's a tried and tested method, and it works.

I promise you that if you follow my suggestions, you will be able to leave within a year, with only slight modifications to your current lifestyle. Above all, you won't waste time making the same mistakes I made initially. It's natural that you might be afraid to give up your current lifestyle. I was, too. I thought about it for three years before deciding to leave. I was afraid of losing my job and my savings. In reality, I was afraid of change. I now realise that the reason for that strong fear was completely in my head. There was nothing stopping me. If I could go back, I would leave immediately. I wouldn't waste time pondering if it was or wasn't the right thing to do.

American actor Sterling Hayden came to the same conclusion way before me. In his autobiography, *Wanderer*, he wrote:

"I've always wanted to sail to the South Seas, but I can't afford it. What these men can't afford is not to go. They are enmeshed in the cancerous discipline of "security". And, in the worship of security, we fling our lives beneath the wheels of routine, and before we know it, our lives are gone.

What does a man need really need? A few pounds of food each day, heat and shelter, six feet to lie down in and some form of working activity that will yield a sense of accomplishment. That's all in the material sense, and we know it. But we are brainwashed by our economic system until we end up in a tomb beneath a pyramid of time payments, mortgages, preposterous gadgetry, playthings that divert our attention for the sheer idiocy of the charade. The years thunder by, the dreams of youth grow dim where they lie caked in dust on the shelves of patience. Before we know it, the tomb is sealed.

Where, then, lies the answer?

In choice. Which shall it be: bankruptcy of purse or bankruptcy of life?"

Don't be someone who misses lifetime opportunities by wasting too much time thinking whether they're good or bad. Act now: do it right away.

Each chapter of this book will clearly explain what to do. How to set your budget, find the money for the trip, which shipping companies to contact, which documents you need and how to obtain them. I describe life on a cargo ship, including interviews with people who have experienced it. You will find advice on how to cope if you are vegetarian, vegan or have specific food intolerances.

Take your life into your hands, now. Enrich it with a new adventure and keep growing.

Chapter 1

Why a trip on a cargo ship

Voyages are the ones you take by sea, on ships, not on trains. The horizon has to be empty and divide the sky from the water. Nothing should be around and immensity should bear down from above. Then it's a voyage.

Erri De Luca, *The Day Before Happiness*

A journey that will change your life

If we all had the luck to observe our planet from space, we would see it mostly blue, with white tinges around the poles and some big brownish islands dotting the surface. The blue is predominant because 71% of our planet's surface is covered by water. Nobody can really call himself or herself a traveller if they haven't at least once experienced a journey by sea.

Why choose a cargo ship instead of a cruise ship? Because a voyage on a cargo ship is more of an adventure than a simple vacation, as it would be on a cruise ship. It's both more raw and more real. It's not a hotel on the waves.

Probably, like me, you are also a person who loves adventure and dreams about journeys that lead to the discovery of new places and people of a different culture. Journeys that will free you, making you *feel* free. The endless ocean beckons, where your gaze gets lost in the horizon. It's an odyssey that comes closest to the true sense of freedom.

This is where the idea of a trip on a cargo ship came from.

When we were little, our parents told us to study because "What you learn will never be taken away from you." The same concept can be applied to travel, too. Travelling, however, has something more. It's not only instructive but also an experience. And, a journey on a cargo ship will fill you with experiences and memories that no one will be able to take away from you.

You will always remember the feeling of living in a cabin, above the sea, drinking coffee and eating bread and jam in the morning while your thoughts meander towards infinity as your eyes scan the mesmerising blue yonder. You will remember the nights when the waves rocked you to sleep, together with the hypnotic pulsing of the ship's engine.

What I miss most are the morning walks on the deck when, in looking at the sea, I could see nothing and everything at the same time.

I spent many nights observing the stars from the deck; it was one of my favourite pastimes. Astronomers claim that it's possible to see around six thousand stars from Earth with the naked eye. Almost two thousands of these can be seen from basically everywhere, given the right atmospheric conditions. A ship in the middle of the ocean has not just the right conditions, but the perfect ones. The Milky Way sparkles in the sky like a million fireworks.

Unknown ports will introduce themselves to you, revealing their cultures and their daily habits. Most cruise tourists will never get to see these. The interaction with other language speakers at a dinner table will widen your knowledge and points of view. Talking with the crew and with the residents of the small intermediate port towns has reinforced my belief that the majority of people are good and simply want to live their lives peacefully.

It's a journey that invites new friendships. Friendship will be one of the best rewards you receive. Even though you probably won't see most of the people you meet ever again, you'll be aware that somewhere in the world there is someone who is happy to have met you.

"Brilliant! Federico, you have convinced me. I want to do it! But …"

But?

"Well, I've got only two weeks paid holidays, I can't afford to spend ten days on a ship just to get to my destination!"

You're perfectly right. In this case, try to see it from another perspective. If, for you, travelling means having new experiences, meeting new people and seeing places you have never seen, then a trip on a cargo vessel is the ideal choice. The ship is not the means to your destination, but the destination in itself.

The next chapter will show you that there are trips on cargo ships that last as few as ten to twelve days. Once the ship has reached its destination, and you disembark, you will be able to take a plane and go back home in a few hours.

Robert Louis Stevenson, the Scottish author of *Treasure Island*, wrote:

"For my part, I travel not to go anywhere, but to go. I travel for travel's sake. The great affair is to move; to feel the needs and hitches of our life more nearly; to come down off this feather-bed of civilization, and find the globe granite underfoot…"

I think exactly like him.

They say, that when people get on a plane or a train, they can't wait to reach their destination. When you board a cargo ship, you don't leave it so eagerly; you won't want to get off at all.

A voyage on a cargo ship is something exciting, and within your grasp; whether you are a single person, a couple, or a family with children. It's a great adventure that can be experienced by everybody. You only need to have the right information and to follow a method that allows you to make the proper arrangements perfectly.

What is a cargo ship?

Many people's minds associate journeys in a cargo ship with the past, like for those who (now the age of great-grandparents) left the Old-World when very young, sailing towards the USA, Canada, South America or Australia in search of fortune. Still today, the modern cargo ship is the 'sea camel' that crosses the oceans.

The majority of people ignore the fact that shipping generates 90% of worldwide trade. This means that if you look up from reading this and peer around you, nearly everything you see has crossed the sea on board a cargo ship. The shipping of your $90 TV costs around $9. For a $1 can of soft drink, it's around 10c. Transport via cargo ship is so cheap that for Scottish companies it's more economically sound to send their cod to China, have it filleted there, and then have it sent back than to have the job done locally!

Cargo ships transport everything from cars to bananas and from petrol to the flip-flops you wear at the beach. Some of these ships accept paying passengers on board, but usually not more than twelve people. Others not even five. Today, nobody pays for their passage on a cargo ship by working on it. Cash is the currency.

There are four types of cargo ships that carry passengers:

- Container ships: Their entire load is composed of containers that are then carried to their final destination by truck or by train. These ships transport the majority of international commercial goods;
- Bulk Carriers or Bulkers: They carry unpackaged food and material such as grain, ore, coal;
- Ro/Ro Carriers (Roll-on/Roll-off): They transport all types of vehicles, like cars, trucks, buses, bulldozers;
- Coastal Trading Vessels or Coasters: These carry post and occasionally, passengers. They sail from large and small ports along the coast or along rivers and canals.

Container ships and Ro/Ro Carriers accept passengers more easily. The former, though, offer a wider choice of itineraries. I have travelled on containers and therefore, in this book, I shall concentrate more on these types of cargo ship.

Five myths about cargo ship voyages to dispel

When I talk to folks about my experience on cargo ships, certain questions keep coming up. I have decided to dedicate this section of the book to answering these questions and thus dispel five myths about travelling on cargo ships.

Myth no. 1: It's very expensive!

Many people think that travelling on cargo ships is only for wealthy people. The trip may last several weeks, and because of this, people believe it will cost a lot of money. In reality, as we shall see in the following paragraphs, on balance, the cost is within just about everybody's reach.

Myth no. 2: You have to work on board.

Wait a moment. You are paying for your ticket, and you have to work too? No. When you book a place on a cargo ship, you become an effective passenger. You do not have to work on board. That's what the crew is paid for.

Myth no. 3: You have to sleep inside the containers.

Containers are enormous boxes used for carrying goods. Whether people ask this question to tease me or not, initially, some people genuinely thought I had slept inside the containers with the merchandise! It's actually very different. Cargo ships' passengers are provided with very spacious cabins, even bigger than the ones you find on cruise ships.

Myth no. 4: The food must be awful!

That's another myth to dispel. Sailors work seven days a week for several months in a row. All this time they are away from their family

and friends. Food is an important element to keep the sailors' spirits high. Woe betide if their morale gets low!
Cargo ships have fantastic chefs who prepare different and delicious meals every day. If you think I'm kidding, go straight to the chapter *At table with the Captain* and you'll find out I'm not. On the cargo ship that brought me to South America, I never ate the same dish twice in seventeen days.

Myth no. 5: What do you do all day? You must get bored to death!
Those who have travelled on cargo ships have never written a book, a blog article or a single comment in which they say how boring their trips were. Actually, it's the opposite.

Who is a journey on a cargo ship for?

A journey on a cargo ship suits everybody: singles, couples, families with children, and elderly people. There are only two limitations.
The first one is an age restriction. If you are older than 85, it may be difficult to go on these ships. Shipping companies have an age limit for safety reasons and do not allow people over a certain age on board. The age restriction varies with the shipping company.
The second limitation is regarding pets. Shipping companies do not allow people with their pets on board. If you are thinking about moving to another country via cargo ship and you want to take your pet with you, you may want to contact an international shipping company that deals with this type of transport. Here is the website of

one: www.petmovers.com.

A journey for families with children

Not long ago, I read a comment on Twitter which made me laugh and feel sad at the same time. It went like this:

> "Travelling.
> When single: Peru, Iceland, Burkina Faso, Papua New Guinea.
> When married: Paris, Florence, New York.
> With children: Disneyland, or a well-serviced seaside resort."

As a good friend of mine would say: "Sadness-a-go-go."

Is it really like that? Children should enrich your life, not clip your wings and make you a slave of daily domestic routine.

I have travelled on a cargo ship together with a family. The Pressl family from Austria has four members: Thomas, his wife Andrea, and their two children, Lukas and Felix. Thomas is an engineer for a bicycle company and Andrea works in the public sector. They were travelling to Buenos Aires, from where they were going to spend the following six months travelling around South America by bicycle. The children really enjoyed the ship; it was a new and stimulating experience for them. Here is an extract from an interview Thomas gave me during the trip, to show you that a journey on a cargo ship is a great experience, even with children.

Federico: Thomas, please, tell me about your travel.
Thomas: We started cycling across Europe from our hometown, Salzburg, to Valencia two months ago. In Valencia, we jumped on this cargo ship to cross the Atlantic and reach Buenos Aires, in Argentina. From Buenos Aires, we're going to ride our bikes for six, maybe eight hundred kilometres up to the north, in Uruguay. Then we will cross the Andes and cycle down into Chile, to Santiago. Maybe a little further down south, we will see. So, all together we're going to spend nine months and we'll ride around eight to ten thousand kilometres by bike. That's the plan.

F: Wow! And why did you decide to travel for so long?
T: Because we want to spend more time all together. At home, we usually have to get up early in the morning, and we come home late in the evening. So there isn't so much time.

F: How do you manage it with your job?
T: Oh, it was easy. At work we just said: "We're going!" (laughing) At the beginning, our boss was not that happy, but after the first shock, he agreed, so after these nine months we will be able to return to our job.

F: What kind of bikes do you have?
T: Two tandem bikes. They make life much easier to cycle with the children. The hard thing is that you have very limited space. You know, two people on the same bike. Even one guy by himself doesn't have much space. But the big advantage is that the children are together with

us, and we don't have to worry about where they are. And, if they are tired, cycling remains easy.

F: How much is the load on the bikes?
T: The total weight of Andrea's bike is 70 Kg, mine is 90 Kg. Plus the trailer we are carrying, about 20 Kg depending on the amount of food and water.

F: Do you have any electronic instruments?
T: Yes. Energy is one of the biggest problems on the road. We have solar panels to support our GPS. Without GPS, it's very hard to bring all the detailed maps, you can't carry so much paper with you. So, the GPS is very handy, but it needs power, two AA batteries. The solar panel is used to recharge them. The other electronic stuff is the laptop and the camera.

F: Where do you usually sleep?
T: Our plan is to sleep only in our tent. Until now, between Salzburg and Valencia, we only slept two nights in a small apartment. For the other nights, we have used the tent.

F: How old are the children?
T: The older one, Lukas, is twelve. Felix is seven years old.

F: So, the children will not go to school for nine months. How do you manage it?

T: The school is not a big problem because in Austria it's not that complicated. You just need the agreement from the teacher and the official side, but usually it's not that complicated. If they agree, the only challenge is carrying school books with you. We scanned and put them all in our e-book reader. We are trying to teach them every day, no more than one hour when we are on the road. We compensate this lack of time doing some extra hours during holidays and teaching more hours here on the ship.

F: Is this your first journey with the children?
T: No, it's the second one. In 2006 and 2007, we did a trip by car. We shipped our car to New York, and we drove from New York up to Canada, crossing over to the West coast and then down to Los Angeles. From Los Angeles, we shipped the car on to Australia where we spent six months. So, in total, we travelled for nine and half months and forty thousand kilometres by car.

F: And how old were the children at that time?
T: Felix was three years old, and Lukas was seven.

F: So Felix was really small!
T: Yes.

F: What do your family and your friends think about this journey?
T: Well, it depends. The family, especially Grandma, is suffering because we are not at home, and the children are not at home, for such

a long time. We know she will suffer a lot. We have a very good and close relationship with her, we see her two, three times in a week. It's very hard for her, but she is happy that we are having this adventure.
As for our friends ... hmmm ... I don't know. Maybe some of them are jealous, and others not. Closer ones know that we like to travel, so mostly are very positive. From people we are not so close to we sometimes hear negative comments too.

F: Why did you decide to take a cargo ship instead of a plane?
T: That's a good question! Hmmm ... why did YOU? (laughing) Well, a plane is maybe too normal. We knew that cargo ships carry passengers because we discovered it many years ago. At that time, taking a cargo ship for us was just a strange idea. But then, this idea grew, and one day we said, "Hmmm, travelling on a cargo ship, that could be interesting." And then the next point was, "When we could do it with the children? Because without the children it might be boring!"
So that was our thought when we started to investigate about it. Then we discovered how expensive it was. Also, the travel agency told us, "Don't go with the children on a cargo ship, it's just too boring!"
But we insisted and then we booked the trip.

F: And now what do you think about life on a cargo ship? Is it that boring?
T: No, not boring at all! It's really a great adventure for us. Incredible. The sea in Austria is not that much bigger (laughing). We are not used to such huge boats. Even the first day, just going on board and looking

around was amazing. And then going on the bridge, seeing the machine room...
And all the people on board are so friendly and so nice. There hasn't been a boring day yet. There is something different every day.

As you can see, a journey on a cargo ship is an adventure that your children will definitely appreciate.

A journey for those with a particular diet

If you are vegetarian or vegan or have other dietary requirements, you can still make a journey on a cargo ship.
An official special menu does not exist on board, so with a bit of imagination, you can easily adapt and fully enjoy your adventure.
On one of my trips, I had just started a vegetarian diet, and I must confess that I didn't have the strength and determination to continue during the trip. Looking back, I now realise that the variety of food that was served every day on board would have allowed me to maintain effortlessly my vegetarian diet.
If you have particular food intolerances, for example if you are a person with a celiac disease, you can still find food that will suit you.
Food is an important issue on a cargo ship. This is why I have dedicated an entire chapter to it. I will provide some simple advice to help you enjoy your journey without relinquishing your eating habits or worrying about your diet requirements. I'll also show you how to avoid making the same mistakes I made. That is, I'll show you how to go

through your journey without changing your diet … and with a full belly.

How much does it cost to travel on a cargo ship?

When I tell people how exciting it is to travel on a cargo ship, often their objections are something along the lines of, "Yes, but it must cost a fortune!"

It costs about as much as an ordinary holiday. I can demonstrate this by using a simple example:

Example of a trip on a cargo ship

As an example, let's take a cargo ship setting out from Savannah Port, in the United States, and arriving at Valencia, Spain.

The shipping company Maris Freighter does this route.

The cargo ship used is the MSC Flaminia. It sails from Savannah and arrives in Valencia in thirteen days. It stops at Charleston (US) and Algeciras (Spain) on the way. A single cabin costs $85 a day while a double occupancy cabin costs $90 per person for two.

If you travel on your own, your trip will cost $1,105. You will have to add port taxes to this, which are between one and a couple of hundred US Dollars. The total cost of the ticket then will be around $1,200.

Then you have to include the plane ticket to go back home (in this case Spain-East Coast USA), which costs on average around $560. Total: $1,760 for fourteen days. Everything included.

Do you think that's expensive? OK, let's see what the ticket includes:

- A private cabin with bathroom and window with sea view;
- Three meals a day: breakfast, lunch and dinner. Lunch and dinner are three-course meals, including dessert. Water is included while wine is at the Captain's discretion. This means that on some ships wine is included in the price while on others it isn't;
- The possibility of having coffee or tea at any time of the day (in any case, coffee and tea are served every day in the afternoon);
- Unlimited access to all recreation areas on board, which in the majority of cases include: a sea water swimming pool, a gym, a sauna, a library, a lounge room;
- Fresh air, the opportunity to meet new people and to observe animals such as dolphins, whales and flying fish in their natural environment;
- To live, at last, a dream adventure of your life.

Do you still think it's too expensive?

Chapter 2

Planning the Journey

There is no favourable wind for the sailor who does not know where to go.

Seneca

Three aspects to remember when arranging your journey

Before going into details, I would like to highlight three main considerations that need to be taken into account during the initial arrangements. You have to keep them well in mind because they are important for helping you to fulfil your dream journey.

Point 1: Unexpected circumstances and delays

You are going to sail on a cargo ship where the shipment is the priority, rather than the passengers. For this reason, it is possible that the shipping company tells you one or two months before departure that the sailing date has been changed.

In this case, the company will provide you with one or two alternative dates. Generally, it will be one alternative date before and one after the sailing date you had originally chosen. The new dates may be a few weeks away from the original one.

It can also happen that the duration of the trip will be extended for a few days. Usually, two possible things occur:

- One or two months before you are due to depart, the company informs you that the duration of the trip has changed. Here is one of my experiences for illustration: I had booked a twelve day trip on a cargo ship. Two months before the departure date, they told me that the trip would now last seventeen days. Luckily it wasn't a problem for me, although if I had already bought a plane ticket to come back the day after my supposed arrival, I probably would have lost the plane ticket money;

- During the trip, the time of loading and unloading of the shipment at the ports in between could take longer than expected. If this is the case, the trip will last one or more days longer.

In such an event, the price of your ticket will not change, and there won't be any additional expenses.

Consider this possible eventuality when making the arrangements for your trip. If your job allows you a certain number of days holiday, it's better you inform your manager about the possibility of a last minute change. I suggest having at least five or six additional days in your planned holiday to cover potential delays.

Point 2: Not all the crewmembers will definitely speak English

On cargo ships, the official language is English, but the crew is usually from non-English speaking countries. It often happens that some sailors speak only a little English. When you book your ticket, you can ask which country the ship is from and then get hold of a dictionary of that country's language. For example, if the ship is German, a pocket English-German dictionary may help you communicate better with those members of the crew who don't speak much English. It is also rewarding to learn some new words in a different language.

Point 3: Why are you doing this?

I left this point until last because I think it's the most important, and I'd like you to take some time to reflect on it.

Answering this question is relevant for two reasons. Firstly, because people (family, friends and strangers) may ask you why you want to do such an uncommon trip. Successfully arguing your choice will be the tool with which you can demonstrate how strong your intention to fulfil your desire is. Secondly, once you realise what the reasons that make you want to do this are, you will be more determined to achieve your objective. The following exercise may help you regarding this point:

Exercise: Why are you going?

Step 1: Take pen and paper and write down the reason(s) for you to want to travel on a cargo ship. You don't have to turn it into an essay or a book; a few sentences will do.

Step 2: Hang the paper somewhere very visible (for example on the fridge door) – somewhere often in your sight.

Step 3: Tell your relatives and friends about your intention to do this trip. Tell them why you want to do it and how you are planning it. Letting other people know about it will reinforce the commitment you have made to yourself.

Decide your budget

The first thing to do in the planning is the setting of the budget, that is, how much you intend to spend for the trip. You need to answer two questions, namely:

- How much do you need for a trip on a cargo ship?
- How much are you willing to spend?

The previous chapter has already given you the answer to the first question: the example described showed you that a two week trip on a cargo ship with returning flight costs roughly $2,000. If you are thinking of doing a longer journey, or a shorter one, refer to Table 1 on the following page, where you can find an approximate estimate of various trips. To simplify the calculation, I've estimated a cost of $140 a day all included (including the return plane ticket).

You have to answer the second question yourself. What I can provide you with, once you've set your budget, is a method with which you'll be able to reach your objective, with minimum effort.

Are you ready? OK, let's go!

Duration (in days)	**Cost per person**
10	$1,400
12	$1,680
14	$1,960
21	$2,940
Around world (approx. 90 days)	$8,400

Table 1

If you work full-time with a permanent contract, you have probably got a certain number of weeks paid holiday, and those two, three or four weeks will be included in your salary.

If we consider a minimum net salary of $1,000 per month, we can set an initial budget of:

$1,000 / 20 working days = $50 a day.

This means that if you take two weeks' holiday, you will be able to spend (without taking extra money out of your wallet or changing your habits):

$50 times 10 days holiday = $500.

I haven't taken into account Saturdays and Sundays as they are not usually paid.

With $500 you can afford around five days on a cargo ship.

These calculations lead to some simple conclusions:

- Whatever your job may be, your salary probably won't be enough to pay for your trip on a cargo ship;
- You will have to slightly modify your lifestyle to save the rest of the money you need to make your dream journey come true.

I will now show you a method of helping to save the amount you need without making radical changes to your lifestyle.

The first step is to define a plan that will allow you to save a sum every month or every week towards the "My journey on a cargo ship" fund.

You will have to make some small changes in your spending habits. For example, you may have to give up one or two meals out a week, but in the end, you'll be well rewarded, with interest.

Here's my example: through a job in Italy with a salary of $1,200 per month, I was able to save $15,000 towards my seven month trip to South America in two years: this was about 50% of my net salary. If I managed to do this with a standard pay, you should be able to put aside a much smaller amount in less time without too much trouble.

A proper plan needs to have a termination date, and in your case this will be the date your ship sails. The next chapter will guide you in the choice of a suitable and realistic date of departure. Meanwhile, here are three exercises for slightly modifying your habits:

Exercise no. 1: Making your "My journey on a cargo ship" fund grow

Step 1: Get a money box (also called a piggy bank). A simple glass jar will do. Get a sticker. Have you got one? Good. Write on it: “My journey on a cargo ship” or whatever you want to call your objective and stick it on the money box.

Step 2: Put the money box in a place where you will see it several times a day. For example, on your bedside table, where you’ll see it every morning and every evening.

Step 3: Start by putting at least $10 a week in it.

I know, $10 a week may seem little at this stage. The aim of the exercise is to help you to focus on your dream and gradually modify your habits. This is why I haven’t mentioned opening a bank account to deposit your savings for the trip. You need some physical reminder of the commitment you have made to yourself. Obviously, if you can put aside a bigger amount, even better!

In any case, great goals are achieved through small steps.

Exercise no. 2: The quantitative jump technique

I didn't develop this technique, I learnt it from the book *Efficacia personale* ("Personal effectiveness") by Piernicola De Maria. One widespread idea is that we should improve our results little by little but do it constantly. The quantitative jump offers you a different challenge: How to produce a three-fold result in a third of the time.

For example, if your goal is a $2,000 trip and you decide to save $200 a month, then it will take you ten months to save the amount you need. How could you, instead, manage to save $6,000 in three months? What do you have to do?

These questions will help you see it from a different perspective. It's a different problem-solution modality, called "lateral thinking", which implies an indirect approach and a look at the problem from various angles.

I'll give you two personal examples:

During the planning of my trip, I had decided I would sell my car a year before leaving. This gave me extra income and eliminated the future monthly costs related to car maintenance (insurance, petrol, repairs, etc.).

Another one:

When I decided to move to London, I needed to put aside some initial money to support me while I was settling there. At the time, I was living in Santiago, Chile. To save some money, I went to live with my fiancée's family. Thus, with the costs of renting a place eliminated, I was able to make more savings. Obviously, I didn't live off others, and I contributed to the household expenses. In any case, I was able to save

the money I needed more quickly.
Dedicate 15-20 minutes of your time every day to think about how to obtain the amount you need for your dream journey in a third of the time.

Exercise no. 3: Measure your progress

Many people like planning and are experts at making good resolutions for the future. Who has never heard the famous words, "Next month I'm going to start a diet"? But, in most cases, things don't go according to plan, and the resolution ends in oblivion. The main problem is that people tend not to follow up their plan or resolution, whereas the key to achieving results is actually the regular measurement of your own progress.
In the case of a diet, people might not write down their weight before starting it. They might not also keep track of what they eat or how many kilos they lose in a certain amount of time. Thus, the end of the month arrives, and they can't figure out where they made mistakes. Finding out you have lost one kilo would give you the motivation to keep going.
Nine times out of ten, not keeping track of one's progress is the recipe for failure. So, document your progress! Record what you save each day.
Here's an exercise:
Step 1: Write in a notebook or a computer file the amount you have at that moment for your trip.
Step 2: Set a sum you intend to save each month. For example, you may

decide to save $100 a month.

Step 3: At the beginning of each week, put aside the amount you need to reach the objective of Step 2.

Step 4: Every time you put aside something, record it in your notebook or file.

Remember: the goal and the measurement of your progress go along the same line. You will never know if you are reaching your goal if you don't measure your progress regularly.

Decide the Departure Date

The second step is to decide when you want to leave.

Choose a date well in advance.

The planning of a voyage on a cargo ship has to start at least a year before the sailing date. This is necessary especially for the booking times. There are limited tickets available and, therefore, it's essential to book way ahead. If there are not tickets for the date you have chosen, the company will probably put you on a waiting list.

Naturally, you can start planning your trip even earlier than a year before. The more time you have at your disposal, the easier it will be to save the money you need.

The best time to leave is without doubt spring or summer. If you are planning a trip to another continent or, indeed, around the world, any period of the year is good.

I left Europe for South America in the middle of September, leaving the beginning of autumn behind me and venturing off to meet spring and summer in the southern hemisphere.

The important thing is to set a date right away. It shouldn't be something too vague, projected in some distant and cloudy future.

"Next year," "Next Summer," are predictions that don't mean anything.

"At the beginning of October 2018," or "The 16th of June 2018." These are deadlines that will enable you to define a precise and concrete objective.

Exercise: Set a departure date and commit to it.

Step 1: Get another sticker and write the departure date on it.

Step 2: Put the sticker on your money box. Keep the money box somewhere prominent where you will see it several times during the day. If you haven't got a money box by now, get one before you continue reading this book.

Your dream will rapidly start to become more real.

Choose the shipping company

We shall now see whom you have to contact in order to buy your ticket on a cargo ship. Some shipping companies offer short trips, others give you the possibility of buying an around the world ticket.

You can spend an awful amount of time on the Internet looking for trips on cargo ships and, at the end of the day, you may still not know which one to choose. In my own experience and among that of other travellers, the best shipping companies are Maris Freighter and

Grimaldi Ferries. Trust me. Many people have travelled with them, and nobody has reported any problems.

Let's look at them in more detail.

Maris Freighter is an American company specialised in cargo ship journeys. I have used this company, and I've been treated very well.

You can book your trip on the Internet from their website: www.freightercruises.com.

The site is only in English, and the booking request can be filled in online. The information required on the form is straightforward: Name. Street Address. City, Country, Nationality, Date of Birth, Telephone number and some info regarding the trip you are interested in.

Subsequent communication regarding the booking will be via e-mail. On the website of this book, you'll find booking drafts already filled. You can use them by copying and pasting the necessary information and inserting the date of your departure.

On my website, there is the direct link where to download the forms: www.federicolepri.com

If you want to make more than one voyage at sea, you can join the Maris Travel Club International. The membership is around $60, and you pay only once. As a lifetime member, you get discounts on all bookings. You also receive a periodical bulletin with all the updates on available trips.

The payment of the trip can be made through a bank transfer or credit card.

In general, a 25% deposit is necessary to guarantee the booking. The balance of the payment will have to be made within seven to ten weeks prior to the departure date.

Grimaldi Lines is an Italian shipping company, with an agency specialising in trips on cargo ships.
For a booking, see their website:
www.grimaldi-freightercruises.com.
The site is also in English. The booking request can be made online or by phone. I have personally contacted Grimaldi Lines by e-mail and by phone for my booking and can verify that they have excellent customer support on the phone and via e-mail.
Like Maris, Grimaldi also has a Freighter Club, but membership is reserved for those who have done at least two trips with them. The membership is free and gives you a 5% discount on future trips.
At the end, when I chose to book with Maris Freighter, it was specifically because their ticket for that route was cheaper than Grimaldi Lines at the time.

Choose your itinerary

Now is the moment to decide the itinerary of your trip.
Over the following pages, you will find some examples of available routes. Each route includes:

- An indicative departure date;
- A list of the ports where the ship will stop on the way (the stops last from a few hours to a couple of days);

- The daily cost per person;
- The estimated number of sailing days. Next to the port town there will be an estimated date of arrival. For example, "New York (27)" means that the estimate arrival at New York is the 27th day of sailing. The routes are from Maris Freighter.

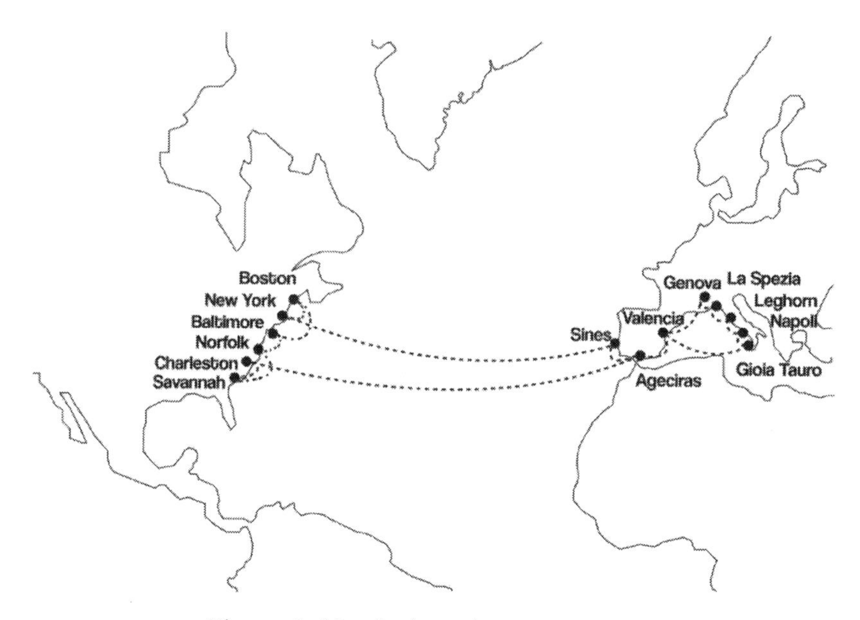

Figure 1: North America and Europe

North America and Europe

The ship MSC Flaminia sets out every six weeks from New York and does a return trip to Europe. These are its stops (see Figure 1):

New York (day 1), Boston (2), Baltimore (5), Norfolk (6), Savannah (8) and Charleston (10), US; Algeciras (20) and Valencia (21), Spain; Gioia Tauro (23), Naples (24), Leghorn (26), La Spezia (27) and Genoa (28),

Italy; Valencia (30), Algeciras (31); Sines (33), Portugal; New York (42). The ship has two 30m^2 suites and one 18m^2 single. The suites cost $90 per person per day, double occupancy while the single is $85.

Europe and Asia

Ships sail every seventy days. Here are their stops (see Figure 2): Trieste (day 1), Italy; Port Said (5) and the Suez Canal (6), Egypt; Jeddah, Saudi Arabia (10); Port Kelang (23), Malaysia; Singapore (25) and Shanghai (33), China; Pusan (36), Korea; Chiwan (40) and Hong Kong (41), China; Singapore (45); Suez Canal (56); Port Said (57); Beirut (59), Lebanon; Trieste (63); Koper (65), Slovenia; Rijeka (68), Croatia; and back to Trieste (70).

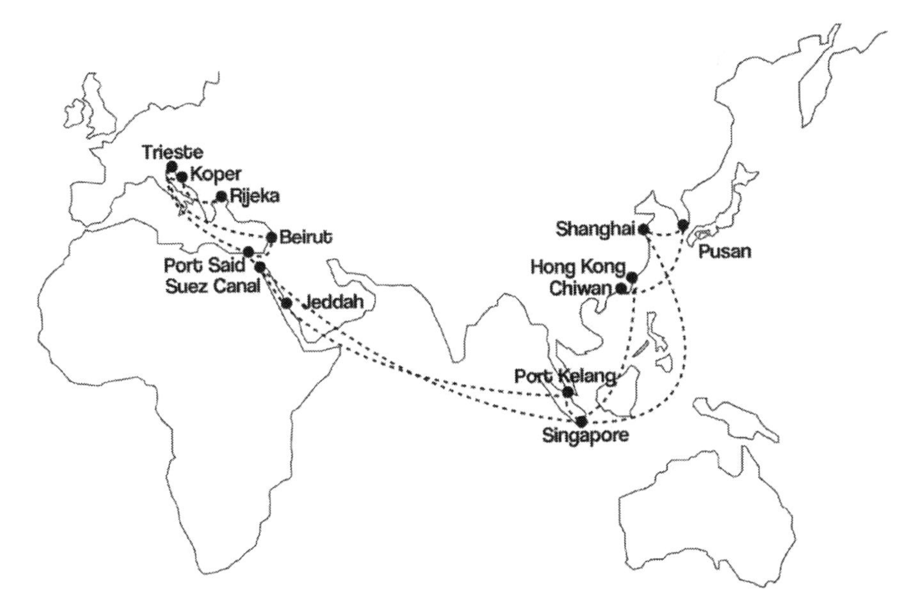

Figure 2: Europe and Asia

On board, there are two 35m^2 and two 23m^2 suites. There are also

20m² single cabins. The suites cost between $90 and $95 per day per person, double occupancy, and the single costs $85.

Europe and South America

Ships sail every week. Here are their stops (see Figure 3):

Tilbury (Day 1), United Kingdom; Rouen (2) and Le Havre (4), France; Philipsburg (13), St. Martin; Port of Spain (15), Trinidad; Cayenne (18), French Guyana (18); Belem (24), Fortaleza (27) and Natal (29), all in Brazil; Algeciras (37), Spain; Rotterdam (41), Holland; Tilbury (42).

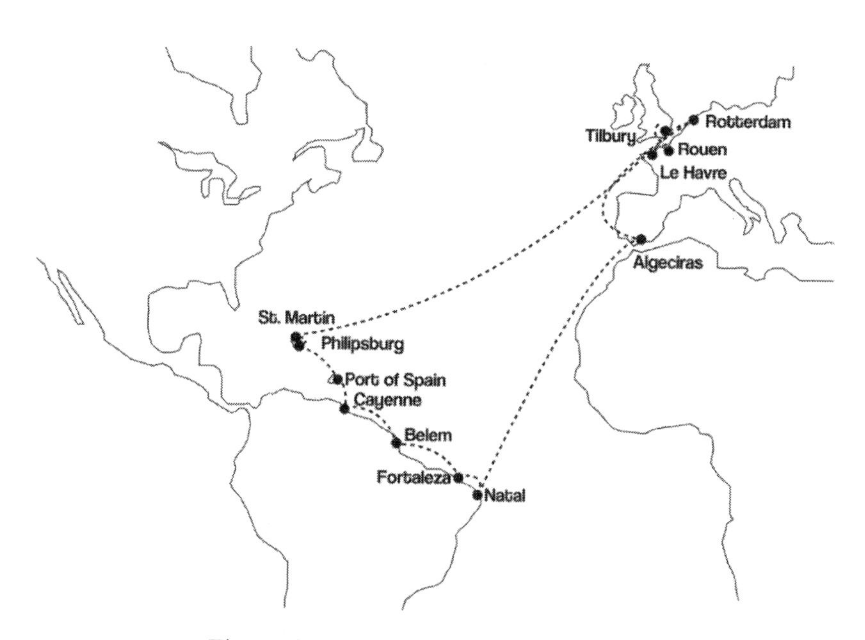

Figure 3: Europe and South America

These ships have 23m² suites, with a price range of $100 per person per day, double occupancy, or $110 for one person.

Europe and Australia

The ships MSG Geneva and Monterey set out for this trip every two months. These are their stops (see Figure 4):

La Spezia (1), Naples (2) and Gioia Tauro (3), Italy; the Suez Canal (7), Egypt; Pointe des Galets (18), Reunion; Port Louis (20), Mauritius; Sydney (34), Melbourne (37), Adelaide (41) and Fremantle (46) Australia; Singapore (55), China; Dubai and Jebel Ali (66), United Arab Emirates; Dammam (68) and Jubail (70), Saudi Arabia; Dubai (72); Salalah (75), Oman; Jeddah (79), Saudi Arabia; the Suez Canal (82); Piraeus (85), Greece; Valencia (88), Spain; Fos sur Mer (90), France; La Spezia (91), Italy.

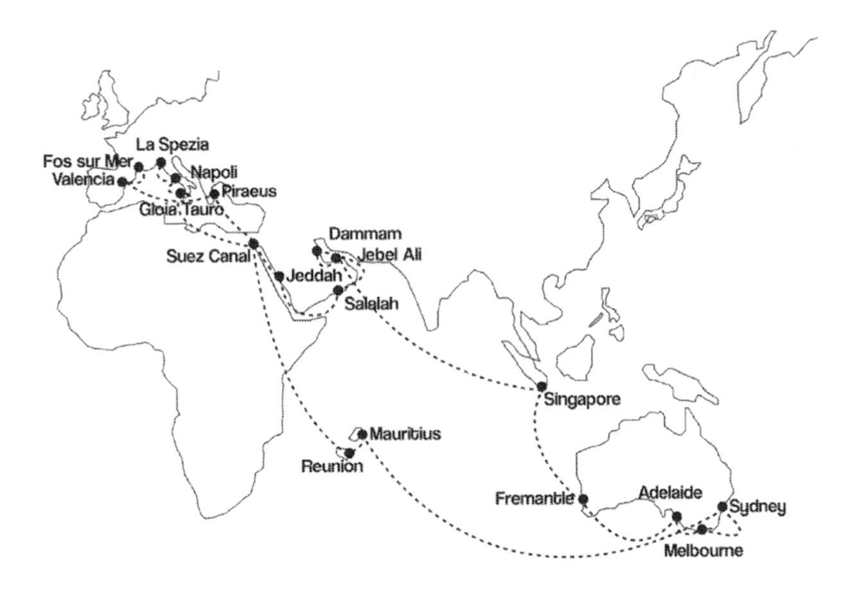

Figure 4: Europe and Australia

The ship has three suites of around 34m^2 and 27m^2. The cabins cost between $90 and $95 per person, double occupancy, or $110 for a single person per day.

Exercise: Decide which route you want to take for your journey

At this point, you have all the information you need in order to choose your route. Do you want to travel to South America the way many European emigrants from the past did? Or, perhaps you want to trace some of Marco Polo's routes and travel to the Far East?

Step 1: Before you continue reading this book, take some time to daydream about which route you would most like to do on a cargo ship.

Step 2: After choosing the route, fetch your money box and get a new sticker and a pen.

Step 3: Write the chosen route on the sticker and attach it to the money box.

Your objective is now taking more solid form.

Decide how long you want to travel for

A journey on a cargo ship may last ten-twelve days for a crossing of the Atlantic, or up to three months for an around-the-world journey.

It all depends on your economic and time possibilities.

If you work on a fixed contract and have around two or three weeks' holidays, and if you include weekends, you probably have a maximum period of around four weeks to use for the journey.

In this case, I suggest you consider a three-week trip, which will include a few days for visiting your ship's destinations.

You can also make use of the accumulation of unused holidays. Determine your situation with your company if you have this option. For example, one of my colleagues from my former workplace was able to accumulate almost two months' holidays in less than two years.

Another opportunity to acquire more time is to work on weekends or public holidays when the company asks for someone, and instead of being paid for those days, claim them as extra holidays, which you can add to your regular number of holidays. There are also companies that will let you take additional unpaid holidays.

Naturally, if you are a professional or a manager, it will be easier to arrange your holiday period with your colleagues or superiors.

As already mentioned, the trip may be longer than expected. Always take this into account and give yourself an additional couple of days. The extra days on board won't cost you anything because in the event of delay the shipping company is responsible for it.

Exercise: Decide the duration of your trip

At last! Choosing the duration of your journey will be the last step in your planning. It mainly depends on the route you have chosen during the previous exercise. Remember that you can always add extra days to your journey for visiting the destination city.

Alternatively, you can choose a ship that travels the same route in less time.

Step 1: Take another sticker and enter the duration of your trip.

Step 2: Put the sticker on your money box.

Necessary documents

Now, for the documents that you will need to travel on a cargo ship. Obviously, the first essential is a valid passport. To avoid hassles, I suggest you ensure that the expiry date on your passport is at least six months after the departure date. For example, if your cargo ship sets out on the 12th of August 2017, your passport should be valid until at least the 12th of February 2018.

Many countries explicitly require tourists to have a passport that is valid for either three or six months after their date of entry. Otherwise, the traveller will have to pay a fine or possibly even be denied entry into that country.

Having a valid passport with all necessary paperwork (like visas) will also enable you to leave the ship and visit the port towns it stops at on the way. There is nothing worse than arriving at, say, the port of Singapore and being refused permission to visit the city because your passport is not "in order".

The other necessary document is travel insurance, which includes recovery and repatriation. If you don't have proper travel insurance, the ship's captain can refuse to let you on board.

The insurance costs will depend mainly on the number of travelling days and you can request further details when you make your booking. Whether you book with Maris or with Grimaldi, their agents will be able to refer you to an associated insurance company. A trip on a cargo ship is uncommon, so it's better and less wasteful to use insurance companies that normally deal with these trips.

The shipping company you book your ticket with will ask you to complete a form certifying that you have a travel insurance policy. You will only have to enter your name and policy number and sign it. You can send it to the company via email, after having scanned it.

On my website of this book (see above), you'll find a sample of this type of form in the Resources section.

Remember: during the booking process, ask the shipping company which insurance agencies to contact for travel insurance.

The third important document you need to board the ship is a medical certificate of good health signed by your doctor. Shipping companies are not obliged to have a doctor on board if there are less than twelve passengers. They require a document guaranteeing that you are in good health before boarding.

When you book your ticket, the shipping company will send you a certificate via e-mail to take to your doctor who will fill it in, sign it and return it to you. This document certifies that you are in good health and fit for travel on a ship.

As soon as you have the certificate signed, scan it and send it to the company.

You can find a sample on my website (see above) of this document, as well. Before you continue reading this book, you should download it.

Remember: the certification must not be older than a month prior to the departure date. For example, if your ship sets out on the 12th of August 2017, you must visit your doctor AFTER the 12th of July 2017. If the certification is older than a month, it loses its validity and you

may have to redo it, or worse, you may not be able to board.
Depending on the route and destination, some vaccinations may be required. In this case, to be able to board, you will need vaccination certification. During the booking process, the shipping company will tell you if you need specific vaccinations for your trip.
Q: Which vaccinations are usually required?
A: To travel on a cargo ship, it's often necessary to have a yellow fever vaccination. This disease is caused by a virus transmitted via mosquito bites and is found in South America and Sub-Saharan Africa. It's a serious disease and has an up to 50% mortality rate.

You can get your vaccination in clinics specialising in tropical travels. This vaccine lasts ten years from the tenth day after the vaccination and must be administered at least a month before the departure date.
The clinic will give you certification; if they don't, you can explicitly request them to provide it.
Remember: keep all certification safely. I suggest you make some copies or scan it and retain it on your computer. The shipping company will ask you a few weeks before your departure date to send them a copy of all certification.

Exercise: Book your vaccinations immediately

If you have decided to go with a cargo ship that requires vaccinations, contact your local specialised clinic as soon as possible and book a visit. This simple operation will completely change your vision. This is a first step which helps confirm both to yourself and to others that you are serious about this journey. From here on it will all be 'smooth sailing'.

What to pack

We are set! Now that you have booked your trip and decided how long it's going to be, you can start thinking about a list of what to pack in your bags.

Here is some good news: the maximum luggage allowed is 100 kg. Much more than what you are allowed on a plane. As usual, the rules of common sense must be applied: obviously, weapons, explosives, dangerous or toxic goods and drugs are not permitted. Moreover, your luggage must not contain merchandise for sale.

Packing your bags is something that will reflect your lifestyle and habits. You know best what you will need during your trip. However, I'd like to give you a list of items that will be useful on board and that you may not have considered.

Some old clothes

Container ships can have soot caused by the smoke of the funnel stack. You can find oily and greasy surfaces on deck. You may also come across wet paint areas. For these reasons, it's better to bring some old T-shirts and pants that you don't use anymore. At the end of the trip, you can leave them on the ship to be used for rags in the engine room. Keep your good clothes for when you get off at the stops to visit the port cities. Remember to take a pair of shoes with you that are easy to put on and easy to take off for around the ship. Slippers and flip-flops are a good idea to take with you to use exclusively in your cabin.

Universal adaptor kit

On cargo ships, sockets, as well as voltage, can be different from your country. Some sockets may not have a grounding hole. In fact, I suggest you bring an adaptor and a voltage converter. You will absolutely need to have an adaptor kit. They are cheap to buy and hardly take up any space at all. You can find them in most electrical shops or online.

The reason for having this is so that you will be able to bring your camera, phone, hair-dryer and so on, and plug them in on the ship. In particular, bipolar adaptor plugs (twin pin) allow the use of tripolar (triple pin) plugs in any two-pole socket: in simple words, this adaptor allows you to connect a three-pin plug into a two-hole wall socket mains (the "Europlug" receiver).

Warning: adaptors 'adapt' only the plug's shape to sockets but do not adapt the voltage.

If your device operates exclusively with the voltage of your country, you may have to buy a transformer kit to change the charge to 220-250V. You can also find these kits in electrical shops or online. The exact term for these transformers is 'mains voltage converter'.

The transformers sold inside travel kits usually work with a current up to and not more than 50W. This means that you can only connect small electrical devices like a mobile battery charger or a camera. In any case, read carefully the instructions and NEVER connect a hair-dryer because the transformer will blow straight away.

If you are not sure about your cabin sockets, you can always ask the captain or a member of the crew.

I suggest you also bring an extension cord in case your cabin doesn't have sockets close at hand.

Earplugs and mask

If you are not used to sleeping on a ship, it may be difficult for you to be able to fall asleep, and any minor noise could make it even more difficult. You can buy good earplugs (like wax ones) at the chemist that are fantastic for eliminating surrounding noises.

Windbreaker jacket and hat

Spending your nights looking at the stars from the ship deck will be one of the most exciting experiences that you'll have during your journey. In cities, it is basically impossible to observe the Milky Way and the constellations. On a ship, in the middle of the quiet ocean, away from light pollution, our galaxy will reveal itself to you in all its magnificence.

With this in mind, I recommend bringing an anorak or windbreaker jacket and a jumper, along with a hat, even if you are travelling in, or towards, a hot part of the globe, or if you are sailing in summer. Out at sea, the temperature can suddenly fall during the night, and on deck there is usually at least a light wind constantly blowing.

Medical kit

Before leaving, prepare a supply of all the medicine that you usually take if you get sick. Cargo ships have an infirmary and base medicines, but it may happen that you are allergic to some medicines. For example, I am allergic to aspirin, a very common medicine, prescribed in many parts of the world for various minor illnesses.

Make a list of all the medicine you take when in need, and a few days before leaving, go and buy them from the chemist.

If you have never been on a boat, buy a packet of pills for seasickness, as well. It's not worth the risk of ruining such a beautiful lifetime experience for one tiny detail, right?

Those books you never had the time to read

As you will see in the chapter about life on board a cargo ship, it will be a very relaxing holiday, with plenty of time to finally be able to read those books you never had the chance to even start.

Chapter 3

The day of departure

There is nothing more beautiful than the moment before the voyage, the moment where the horizon of tomorrow comes to tell us its promises.

Milan Kundera

The day of your departure has finally arrived.

It is possible that the ship sets out one or two days before or after the original date.

At least three days before departure, go to the port and get in contact with the shipping company's Port Office, to receive a confirmation of the departure date. If you don't know how to get in contact with the company's Port Office, ask the shipping company employee who sold you the ticket to give you their phone number.

Once you are in this office, you will be put in contact with the person responsible for dealing with the ship's arrival and departure. Here are some things you should ask them about:

- Confirmation of day, date and time of the ship's arrival;
- Docking Bay (quay) number. This piece of information is very important. It's quite easy to lose your direction in a shipping port, especially if it's big and busy. Knowing your docking bay number is important in case you can't find your ship and you need to ask someone directions;

- An emergency phone number to call in case there are some problems (for example, you can't find your ship's docking bay).

Remember to leave your mobile phone number with the employee you speak to, so you are reachable for anything.

If you are leaving from a foreign port and you don't speak the language, it won't be a big problem. The basic information that you need to determine at the port is the name of your ship (you'll be given this when you book your ticket) and the expected departure date. Usually, proper names have a similar pronunciation in most languages, and with the aid of some universal gesticulation, you should be able to make yourself understood.

I boarded a cargo ship setting out from Barcelona bound for South America and I didn't speak a word of Spanish. The Barcelona Harbourmaster's porter didn't speak a word of English. My dream journey was too important to be impeded by this person. So I didn't give up. Employing all the possible intelligible gestures I could and by slowly articulating the name of my ship, I was finally able to make myself understood and was quickly sent to a person who spoke English.

One last thing: on the day of departure, make sure you have at hand your passport and all the required documentation (as mentioned above).

Now, let's go through the boarding procedures.

At the port

At this stage, the shipping company's office has provided you with all the instructions and information for boarding. In particular, they have given you the exact address of the port and the docking bay number of your ship. As with airports, cargo ports are very well secured places and access is permitted only if you have valid reasons. They can be very big and you can find internal port taxi drivers that will take you directly to the gate of your docking bay.

At the gate, you'll probably come across a guard to whom you will have to show your ticket. Remember, you are in a cargo area, not in a tourist harbour, and people may not behave as you expect. They might pay more attention to merchandise than people; therefore try to be patient. They are not used to seeing passengers wandering around cargo ports. The guard will take you directly to your ship's docking wharf. If your boat has not yet entered the port, you'll have to wait until they call you.

The wait

Once the ship has docked, you'll just have to wait until the loading and unloading process is finished. The guard at the gate will let you know when you can board the ship.

Cargo ports are very busy and often enough, the time of arrival of a ship isn't the expected time. I suggest you ask the guard at the gate every 30-40 minutes for the latest news about your ship's time of arrival. The guard is in contact with the ships docking at the wharves via radio and receives constant updates on their movements.

Prepare for a long wait. Take some food with you and find a comfortable place to sit. Just so you have an idea, my ship was supposed to dock at 11:00 a.m., but I had to wait several hours and did not board until 4:00 p.m.

If your ship is due to dock in the evening, bring something to cover up with you and prepare to wait even all night. Don't worry, you've got this far, and soon you'll be able to get on board your ship!

Boarding

When you board the ship, you'll be surrounded by plenty of movement. The loading and unloading process will not yet be completed and the sailors and stevedores (or "dockers") will be working fast, moving containers and manoeuvring the ship's mooring ropes. It's normal if during this phase they don't pay you any attention. The loading and unloading operations must be done inside a set time, so the ship can leave the dock and make space for the next ship (which will probably already be waiting outside the harbour). A cargo officer will accompany you on board. If you want, you can use the naval custom (as seen in some movies) and say: "I request permission to come aboard, Sir." Naturally, this is not necessary, but it will add some colour to your story when you tell it to your friends and relatives after your return.

On the ship, the cargo officer will introduce you to the crew member assigned to be the passengers' onboard steward. This person will be your contact representative for the whole trip.

Enjoy the moment and congratulate yourself. You are aboard, it's time to celebrate!

Chapter 4

Life aboard

Beyond the East the sunrise, beyond the West the sea,
And East and West the wanderlust that will not let me be

Gerald Gould

Areas of the ship

Some areas on the ship are off limit to passengers. Try to explore the areas you are allowed into as much as possible. Sometimes the Captain himself will offer to take you around to see some places or watch particular operations. Don't reject the offer. I had the opportunity to visit the engine room thanks to the Head Engineer, and it was incredible. On another occasion, the Second Officer asked me to take part in the anchor release operations. Exploring the ship and finding out about daily operations is another way to enrich your journey.

You are aboard a ship and not inside a building; therefore, you won't hear the word 'floor', but 'deck'. On this subject, following is a short guide on how container ships are generally structured. My description starts at the lowest part of the ship and goes to the highest.

Engine Room: Imagine a hot, noisy, dirty, badly lit room. The engine room is tucked deep inside the dark depths of the ship, and it is so noisy that you are obliged to wear ear protection.

It is immense, probably four or five decks high from top to bottom. Inside the engine room, apart from the ship's motor itself and the transmission shaft, there are many smaller motors which provide energy to the other systems of the ship: the electricity system, pumps, refrigeration units, air conditioning, the desalination plant, and many others. The Head Engineer and his team have the heavy responsibility of looking after all of these machines and need to officially note anything that happens in the logbook.

Cargo hold: The area where the ship's containers are stored.

Deck A: On this internal deck you generally find the kitchen, the pantry and the canteen.

Deck B: On this external deck, the inflatable lifeboats are stored at both ends of the passage.

Deck C: In general, this part holds the recreational areas of the ship: swimming pool, sauna and gym. There are also lounge-rooms for the officers and crew.

Deck D: Here there are some of the crewmembers' cabins: chef, boatswain, etc.

Deck E: Here there are the officers', passengers' and engineers' cabins.

Upper Deck: On this level there is the control room. It's similar to a conference room, with the addition of a few computers, printers and other office items.

The Navigation Bridge: It's also simply called "The Bridge". This is the ship's control centre. It contains numerous computers, radars, monitors and onboard systems. The ship is driven via a mini-wheel about 10cms in diameter, or via a *joystick*. There is an area where the nautical world and regional maps are stored, along with a big table on which the actual ship's route is traced. On both sides of the deck, there are two open areas usually known as boardwalks, from where the captain and the pilot can control the ship's movement during docking operations at the port.

"Monkey deck": This is on top of the watchtower. This small area above the navigation deck contains a series of electronic instruments like GPS, radar, communications antennas, and satellite receivers. The name 'monkey deck' probably comes from the nineteenth century and is due to the prevailing necessity for sailors to climb the mainmast like monkeys to reach this small area on top of it. It was necessary to climb up there to take the readings for the celestial navigation or to spot other vessels, icebergs, reefs, land and pirates.

Your cabin

Passenger cabins are spacious, and as you have seen, they are usually on the upper deck. These cabins were used by officers before the current development of technology reduced the size of the crew necessary for cargo ships.

The cabins are usually bigger than those you find on cruise ships and they have all the comforts: TV, DVD player, stereo and a small fridge.

While aboard, I had the possibility of visiting the cabins of some officers, and I can assure you they are practically the same as the ones given to passengers. The latter are considered respected guests on a cargo ship.

Your cabin will be cleaned once a week by the steward. The linen and towel changing is all included in the service. On some cargo ships there is a daily cleaning service. Remember that the steward can only clean your cabin when you are not in it. When it's time for the cleaning, the steward may kindly ask you to leave the cabin. Obviously you can stay in your cabin if you wish, but in this case, the cleaning won't be done. The bigger cabins have a small living space with armchairs or a couch, a table or a desk.

The other passengers

During your journey, you may get to know other passengers. Cargo ships can carry up to six or eight people.
Since travelling this way is an uncommon thing to do, they will probably be people with a similar open mind and character. Cargo ships seem to have the privilege of putting together like souls, with similar habits and ways of thinking. The people you meet will enrich your life and enable you to enjoy your journey even more. Make the most of it!

The crew

The ship's crew is principally divided into officers and seamen. The majority of officers are from Europe: Germans, English or Poles. Being an officer is quite a job. Their contract is of the 3+3 or 4+2 type. In the first case, it means three months aboard followed by three months holiday while in the second case, it's four months aboard and two on holiday. When I think about my past twenty years of paid

holidays I get the shivers.
The ordinary seamen are usually Filipino, Bengali, Chinese or Indonesian. Contrary to the officers, their contract provides them with less holiday time, and these are generally unpaid. Most of them have a nine-month contract, which means doing an around the world trip three times, working seven days a week and without seeing home once in these nine months.
Whatever cargo ship you have the opportunity to travel on, there's a good chance the seamen will principally be Filipinos. People from the Philippines are very friendly and happy, and I was pleasantly able to find out about their culture during my travels. They generally speak decent English, are very religious, and can manage to convey an incredible sense of happiness. Despite the economic differences between the ordinary seamen and the officers, the former are without doubt the more cheerful and calm amongst the crewmembers.
Before leaving, try to learn a few Tagalog (Filipino) words or expressions. This will pleasantly surprise them and help break the ice more easily. To encourage you in this little task, I've added some typical phrases that you can learn and use on board in Table 2.

If you like taking photos, bring your camera and, if possible, also a small printing machine. Pictures of onboard activities and work will be very appreciated. You can even use an old Polaroid. The seamen will be very thankful if you give them photos of themselves to keep or to send to their family.
You can also take a picture of your boat before leaving, to keep with

Hello	Hai
Good morning	Magandáng umaga
How are you?	Kumustá?
Fine	Mabuti
And you?	Ikáw?
What's your name?	Anó ang pangalan mo?
My name is...	Ang pangalan ko ay...
Pleased to meet you	Nagagalák akóng
Thank you	Salamat po
See you later	Sige
Goodbye	Babay
Goodnight	Magandáng gabi

Table 2

you when going to visit the port cities where the ship stops on the way. It might become useful in case you get lost. For example, you could show it to a taxi driver if he or she doesn't understand where you want to go.

Working on a cargo ship is not an easy life. The sailors spend a good part of their working life away from home. Their job is heavy and dangerous and often done in foreign countries, where they can't access basic services like, for example, healthcare. Apart from the old saying "women aboard bring bad luck," it's not surprising the fact that, in general, the crew of a cargo ship is exclusively made up of men.

On the cargo ship I took to go to South America, however, the fourth officer was a woman, the only one among a crew of thirty members. Marika (I've used a fictitious name for privacy reasons) was from Poland, and I took the opportunity to interview her.

Federico: Why did you choose this job?
Marika: I chose this job because of my passion and because of my respect for the sea. I spent my childhood in a small town in the northern part of Poland, close to the sea. Every day I used to walk along the beach with my dog. I felt so free and comfortable when looking at the water and the seagulls. I wanted to see the sea and the ships every day of my life.

F: Which is your grade?
M: I am the 4th Officer, but I already have a 3rd Officer's license. I was 3rd Officer in another company, but in this one [NSB Freighter Cruises] the rule is that if you want to be 3rd Officer, you must sail twice as 4th Officer. Finally, on my next voyage, I will be 3rd Officer.

F: What are the duties of a 4th Mate?
M: On the ship the 4th Officer takes care of security. When we are on the open sea, I have to stay on the bridge with the 3rd or the 1st Mate. When the ship is at the docks, I have to check deck operations. I also have to prevent security incidents on board. For example, broken padlocks to restricted areas. I am the commander of all ISPS drills. I teach the crew how to react when there are bombs or drugs on board and how to act when we have a piracy alarm.

F: How long have you been doing this job?

M: I began this adventure during my studies in 2004 [8 years prior].

F: What has been your longest journey on a cargo ship?

M: My longest trip was 5 months and 25 days.

F: What is your typical day like?

M: I wake up at 7.30 in the morning. I have breakfast and then I do a watch on the bridge from 8 to 12 in the morning and from 8 to 12 at night. When the ship is in the docks, I have to be on watch on deck from 4 to 8 in the morning and from 4 to 8 in the afternoon.

F: Do you miss having other women around?

M: Yes, often I miss the presence of other women. It would be more comfortable if I were not the only woman on the ship...but now I'm used to it.

F: Have you ever felt uncomfortable?

M: There have been a lot of situations when I haven't felt comfortable. Everything depends on the crew. If I have some problems, I just keep away from the person causing these uncomfortable feelings.

F: What does your family think about your job?

M: My family is proud of me and they understand my passion for the sea. Of course, they are worried, but they know that everything will be all right.

F: Do you have a boyfriend?

M: Yes, I have a boyfriend. He is also an officer, but his grade is higher than mine, he is a Chief Mate. We work for two different companies. It's very hard to find a job together on the same ship, but we are trying to somehow join the same crew and ship at the same time and go back home together. I love him very much, and I know that, for him, I am the only girl in the world. Of course, it's very hard because we can't see each other for 4-5 months ... but our love is strong, and I'm sure that nothing will destroy our relationship. He is very proud of me, and he knows that this job is my passion.

F: What do you miss most when you are away at sea?

M: When I am at sea, I miss walking with my boyfriend. I miss my family too but fortunately time runs fast on the ship. I can send emails, and I can call my family every day, so it's not that hard.

F: And when you are at home?

M: When I am at home I miss the view of the ocean, and I miss looking at my favourite animals: the dolphins and the gulls that fly over the boats.

Leisure time

Since the crew has to spend several months aboard, cargo ships are provided with different forms of leisure activities.

There is always a recreation room on the ship. Officers and seamen have separate recreation rooms. These are spacious and usually equipped with a TV, DVD player, a number of armchairs and sofas, a gaming table, a fridge and a small bar. As a passenger, you have the right to use the officers' room.

On cargo ships, there is also a gym for the crew to keep in good shape when not working. Usually, the gym has a stationary bicycle, fitness equipment and an exercise ball. As with the recreational room, you can use the gym as well. By using the gym, you'll have the opportunity to make conversation with the crewmembers and get to know them better.

Aboard you can also find a sauna, a ping-pong table and a swimming pool with seawater. The different types of recreation facilities vary with each cargo ship; therefore, you may want to ask about them when you make your booking. On the cargo ship I travelled on, there was a basketball hoop on the external deck.

If you get on well with one or more crewmembers, you'll be able to spend some time with them when they are off duty. If they seem a bit unfriendly to you, don't take it personally. On cargo ships, the distinctions between officers and seamen are quite clear, and often the latter prefer to keep to themselves and not mix with the officers (as a passenger you may be considered to all effects an officer).

Another activity that you are able to experience aboard is to spend many nights looking at stars on the deck. I suggest being on the deck just after sunset when the sunlight has not completely disappeared and

the brightest stars are appearing. At night, you will be able to fully admire the Milky Way, which is today, in our cities, a vague memory.
Sailors have a good knowledge of stars, and you might find someone willing to give you an improvised short lesson in astronomy on site. In the past, being able to sail without electronic equipment was fundamental for sailors. The constellations and the sextant were the only necessary instruments. Today it's different, computers and GPS do all the work.
One night, Jens, the captain of the ship I was travelling on, told me that the ability to use the sextant is still necessary and told me a story to show how. In the nineties, the US held exclusive global control of GPS, and during the Gulf War, the Americans decided to switch it off for military reasons. At the time this happened, Jens was in open sea. With the ship's GPS system off, he was able to maintain his route thanks to the sextant and the stars.
You can also spend your time on deck observing the sea's inhabitants: whales, dolphins and flying fish amongst the best known.
Flying fish can be found in all warm waters around the world. They emerge from the water with a pulse of their fins, and some species can fly for up to thirty seconds and as high as one metre. Their flying is a way of escaping underwater predators.
If you are lucky, you will see seabirds like the Manx Shearwater. These birds enjoy gliding and take advantage of the wave of air pressure created by the ship's mass. The Manx Shearwaters spend most of their life offshore and move near the coast only to nest.
One day during my trip, I was sitting on one of the benches situated on

the external deck, waiting for the washing machine to finish my laundry and observing the sea. It wasn't the first time I had been doing that, but that day something magical happened to me.
Suddenly I saw it. A dolphin. Hang on; two dolphins. Three dolphins. An entire school of dolphins! I know that many readers have probably had encounters with dolphins swimming near the coast or in captivity, but I had never seen so many, especially so close. They were playing, doing summersaults and diving back into the water. It's quite rare to feel the energy of Mother Nature in all its raw magnificence. That day I really felt it, and today still, I thank myself for having done that trip by ship.

The Ceremony of Crossing the Equator

If you can, I suggest you choose a route that crosses the Equator. This might give you the opportunity of witnessing and taking part in a beautiful experience in the life of sailors: the ceremony of crossing of the Equator.
If there is a sailor on board who has never crossed the Equator before, the captain organises a ceremony to celebrate the occasion. According to tradition, this is indeed an initiation rite for the sailor in question. The other crewmembers paint his face and make him drink a disgusting sort of slop made of rice, fish, and God knows what else. After the ceremony, the crew celebrates all together. The difference between officers and ordinary seamen no longer exists; they are all part of the same family of people who dedicate their lives to the sea.

If you are lucky enough, the captain will issue a certificate of Crossing The Line to you as well. On the certificate there will be something written, more or less like this:
"To all sailors, wherever they may be. To all sirens, whales, sea snakes, sharks, fish, crustaceans and all other inhabitants of the sea. We declare that [your name] has been initiated into the solemn Ancient Order of the Mysteries of the Deep, and Thus, from hence he must be paid due respect and honour."

Communication with the outside

On the open sea, communication with the outside world is practically non-existent. Take advantage of this to disconnect yourself from daily matters and relax. The constant ringing of your mobile phone, and the daily calls from work or from your in-laws will be distant memories.
However, don't worry, if you need to contact someone, all cargo ships have satellite phones and Internet connections for the crewmembers.
The disconnection I'm talking about regards those cargo ships that cross the ocean to reach another continent. In other cases, cargo ships sail near the coast, at a distance that will possibly still allow your mobile to work. Nevertheless, it is possible that you won't be able to communicate with your friends and family for several days. Make sure they know this before you leave.
If you really need to call someone when out at sea, you can always use the ship's satellite phone. It'll be very expensive, though. You can buy $50 prepaid cards (or similar amounts) from the captain, which will

give you five or ten minutes calling time. The exact cost of these cards depends on the phone company.
For ordinary communications, some ships provide access to emails. Internet connection is via satellite and it's very expensive. E-mail messages (sent and received) must be without emoticons, images or attachments.
If your voyage lasts more than ten days, the ship will surely make stops on the way, and you can easily call friends or relatives from the port cities you visit.

Time zones

The world is subdivided into 24 time zones with reference to the Greenwich Meridian (0°) in the UK. If you are travelling westwards, you usually move your watch back one hour any time you cross a time zone. If you are travelling eastwards, you move it forward.
When we cross several time zones in a short period of time, for example when travelling by plane, we might experience jet lag and reach our destination sleepy, tired, or confused.
If you usually suffer jet lag after a long distance flight, here's some good news: you won't suffer it travelling on a boat!
A boat moves much slower than a plane and in the worst of cases, the time zone changes twice in a row for two consecutive days. It means you have to change your clock the first day and then the second day. Your body will have much more time to adapt than when travelling by plane.

You do have to adapt to the changes of mealtimes and wake-up time, though (I call it *ship-lag*), but it's nothing compared to all the nuisance of a proper jet lag.

Quite a difference, don't you think?

If you are travelling with your children, they might be more affected by the changing of time zones. The Pressl family gave me some practical advice to cope with this, and I pass them on:

- Make sure the children have a proper meal before going to bed: one of the things that wake them up at night during the changing of times is actual hunger. If their stomach is convinced that it's lunchtime, it'll send signals that are difficult to ignore. If the children wake up in the middle of the night hungry, how can you manage to put them back to sleep? If they eat something before going to sleep, even if they are not hungry, it should prevent this problem;
- Keep up routine: if at home your children are used to having a story read to them before going to sleep, don't change this habit during your trip. The familiar routine will help them relax and fall asleep untroubled;
- Keep an eye on afternoon naps. It happens to adults too: your eyes feel heavy, you just lay your head on the pillow for a moment, and you fall into a deep sleep for three hours. Come the evening, you can't close your eyes. In children, this process is accentuated. Limit their afternoon naps to a few minutes, at least for the first two or three days, so they can adapt to the new time zone more quickly.

Clothes

On a merchant ship, the password for clothes is 'casual'! T-shirts, jeans and training shoes are perfect.
During the journey, the weather might change. Bring something warm to wear on the deck and for when you get off the boat.
If your clothes get dirty, don't worry. All merchant ships have a laundry that you can use. The washing machine uses unsalted distilled water, and it needs very little detergent. You will find a dryer and an iron/ironing board as well.
Finally, some common rules exist which it would be best to follow. For example, the captain, the officers and the crew do not appreciate passengers entering the deck or wandering around the ship wearing only a swimming costume. To be safe, just ask the captain when you board the ship if there are any particular rules regarding what you should/shouldn't wear and where.

Stops

When the ship approaches a harbour, it can't simply go straight to its wharf to dock. Each port has its own characteristics and challenges which need to be taken into account for the safety of navigation. Currents, tides, sandbanks, naval traffic and underwater objects are just a few of the risks that the ship's pilot must not underestimate.
For such reasons, before entering the harbour, the captain (or an agent of the company) informs a port officer about the ship's imminent arrival. This port officer will send a local pilot, familiar with local

conditions, aboard the ship, who will subsequently guide the ship safely into the port of its docking. This procedure is done no matter what the conditions of the sea are. Often, when the sea is rough, the pilot has to reach the ship by helicopter. The same procedure applies when the ship leaves the port.

Sometimes the port is full, and there are no free docks for the arriving ship. Other times the weather is so bad that docking is impossible. In these cases, the captain drops the anchor a few miles from the harbour, and they wait. For short delays, the captain might choose to sail his ship around in circles until a docking wharf is available.

The stops during the trip may last from just a few hours (leaving you no time at all to visit the local city) to a maximum of 48 hours. A cargo ship may also arrive at one stop at seven in the evening, load and unload all night, and then leave at seven o'clock the morning after. In these cases, it would be very unlikely that you have the time to visit the place.

If you intend to get off the boat to go and visit the port city, you have to inform the captain a few hours ahead. The captain will call an officer of the port police, who will come to check your documents. If your papers are all in order, they will call you a port taxi to take you into town. You'll have to pay for the taxi, and you'll have to take into account this extra cost when deciding to get off the boat. If the port city you want to visit is big, I suggest you ask the taxi driver his or her phone number to avoid possible delays if you can't find a taxi when it's time to go back to the ship. You can also agree with the taxi driver to meet you again at a certain time.

The captain, the officers and the port agents can give you advice on what to visit in the city, but don't count too much on it. Get the information you need ahead and find out more about the cities during the trip.

If you are worried about getting lost while visiting a port city, you can record the direction you are taking on your mobile phone's voice recorder, or you can take pictures or film with your digital camera, so you have a record of your movements. This will make your return to the ship easier.

Try to be flexible. It may happen that some of the stops are cancelled at the last minute. The only certain thing is… uncertainty! Expect the unexpected. After all, it's an adventure!

Chapter 5

At Table with the Captain

Water, Energy and Food. You must be frugal. You cannot have the opulence of the everyday at sea.

Giovanni Soldini (solitary navigator)

Contrary to common opinion, on cargo ships you eat very well. The only thing to point out is that aboard there are not special menus for particular diets. If you have any special dietary needs (for example, vegetarian or vegan), let the shipping company know when you book your ticket. If the company tells you that the ship menus don't include special diets … well, don't despair! As you can find in the following pages, the menu on board is varied and balanced. If you want, you can even pack some soy burgers or other foods you may want to eat in your bag (remember you have a fridge in your cabin). When on board, you can ask the chef if now and then he can cook the food you brought on board for you.

As a passenger, you have the right to eat in the same room and at the same time as the captain and his officers. This is a great opportunity to chat and get to know them. Give them the possibility to tell you sailors' stories and about their life at sea.

During meal times, a steward serves you. This is the same person who takes care of the cabin and the passengers in the best way possible. Tips are not compulsory, but etiquette expects a daily tip of around $4 -

$5 or equivalent. The steward will be very grateful.
You can choose to eat with the seamen instead of the officers, although on some ships this is not permitted. If you do this, you'll have to help yourself, buffet-style.
Wine is at the captain's discretion. On some ships it's already included, on others it's not. If it isn't included, you can always bring some bottles with you when boarding, or buy it on the ship, as we'll see below.
Remember: If you seem to eat more than at home … that's normal! Scientific studies have demonstrated that the combination of wind, salt and iodized water stimulates people's metabolism and this why you feel hungrier. The effect usually only lasts a few days until the body adapts to the changes.

Mealtimes

Meals are served in the officers' dining room three times a day: breakfast, lunch and dinner. The captain or steward will tell you the mealtimes. In general, breakfast is served at 7:30 a.m., lunch at 12:30 p.m., and dinner at 18:30 p.m. At 10 o'clock in the morning and 3 o'clock in the afternoon, there is usually tea or coffee time accompanied by a light snack.
Aboard some cargo ships, Sunday and Thursday tea times are usually accompanied by an exquisite cake specially prepared by the chef. "Why on Thursday?" you may ask.
The first time I went on a cargo ship I asked this myself, too.
This is what the third officer answered: "Since sailors work very hard

on a cargo ship, they have the right to one extra Sunday during the week: Thursdays."

Not bad, right?

Remember: it's your duty to respect the ship timetables and to adapt to the crew's habits. If you arrive late to a meal, probably the food will no longer be served to you.

What you eat on board

Since meals are for people who work hard all day, they are generous and nutritious. The chef's cooking will definitely fill you up.

You will be served all kinds of food and dishes from different countries. I repeat, on a cargo ship the quality of the food is one of the most important things. The crew must be in good form and, above all, happy. Good food can be an excellent form of mood therapy in these circumstances.

Meals are composed of a first course, second course and dessert. You have two choices for each course. Here's an example of what you can find on a menu:

Breakfast

Scrambled eggs, chicken frankfurters, cereals, fruit juice, milk, coffee, tea, fresh bread, jam and butter;

or

Baked beans, bacon, cereals, fruit juice, milk, coffee, tea, fresh bread, jam and butter;

or

Meat cold cuts, cheese, cereals, fruit juice, milk, coffee, tea, fresh bread, jam and butter.

Lunch

Green salad, soup of the day, baked pork chops, oven cooked potatoes, cauliflower, bread, butter, mineral water, gelato, tea or coffee;

or

Bean and legume soup, green salad, steak and chips, aubergines, bread, butter, mineral water, apple pie, tea or coffee;

or

Greek salad, green salad, beef steak and vegetables, chips, fried aubergines, bread, butter, mineral water, cream custard, tea or coffee.

Dinner

Green salad, legumes soup, beef in barbecue sauce, potatoes, green beans, cheese, cold cuts, bread, butter, mineral water, fruit, tea or coffee;

or

Green salad, pasta with marinara sauce, teriyaki chicken, potato salad with calamari, mineral water, banana cake, tea or coffee;

or

Soup of the day, green salad, spaghetti carbonara, grilled chicken with boiled potatoes, cod cuts, cheese, bread, mineral water, fruit cake, tea or coffee.

The drinking water is seawater which has gone through a process of distillation. The seawater is brought to 80° Celsius with the heat of the engine and the steam is condensed back into water. It's completely safe to drink, and it's used to provide the bathroom water too. Being devoid of all the minerals usually present in land water, it's quite bland and tasteless to drink.

The sample menu I have given above, shows how varied and quite rich meals can be, thus giving you the possibility to eat satisfactorily even if you are on a particular diet.

Five tips for Vegetarians, Vegans and Celiacs

Here are five tips to help you enjoy your mealtimes better in case you are vegetarian, vegan or a person with a celiac disease.

Tip no. 1

During the booking process, tell the shipping company you are on a specific diet. Clearly ask if it will be possible to have special menus. They may answer that it's not possible. But it's always best to try.

Tip no. 2

When you are aboard, ask if any of the crewmembers has requested a vegetarian, vegan or celiac diet. If someone is actually following the same diet as you, you can ask the steward to have the same as his or her dish at mealtimes. The chef will have to prepare it for one person in any case, and it shouldn't be a problem to make two portions of the same stuff.

Tip no. 3

Don't let food go to waste. Wasting food is shameful, especially on board a ship. When you are asked to choose between the available courses, tell the steward what you can't or don't want to have on your plate. For example, if the second course is grilled meat with salad, tell the waiter you only want the salad. Thus, the meat won't get wasted, and you'll get a full plate of salad. Also, the food you do want to eat won't touch the food which you don't want to eat.

Tip no. 4

Before leaving, prepare a bag full of food that you want to eat on board during the trip. In your cabin, there will be a small fridge to store the food you wish to take with you. Unlike when travelling by plane, the good thing about travelling on a cargo ship is that no one will check your luggage when boarding. And, if you are still hungry after a meal, you'll still be able to go back to your cabin and have a secret snack!

Tip no. 5

Offer to cook! When you get to know the captain and his crew better, you may ask if you can cook once. You can propose a dish typical of your country (they don't need to know beforehand that it'll be vegetarian, or whatever). During one of my trips, I offered to prepare pizza for everybody. It was a fun experience, and I even learnt some cooking tricks from the chef.

The 'slop chest'

If you leave the table hungry, you can buy some food from what on board is called a 'slop chest'. It's a kind of shop that sells a few things to passengers and the crew. The origin of this use is from the French, and in the past it was used for a chest full of the captain's clothes that he sold to the crew to replace their worn ones.

At the slop chest, you won't find only food, but also other items you may need during the trip. It's a kind of duty-free to take advantage of when the ship is outside any national territorial boundaries. In Table 3 there are some things you can find inside a cargo ship slop chest with an idea of their price.

If you want to buy something, tell the steward, who will bring you the things directly to your cabin. The items sold in a slop chest are not always the same for all cargo ships, and sometimes it varies on the same ship too. If the wine is not included in your meals, the slop chest becomes a handy choice, and you can bring your bottle of wine to the table with you.

Remember: the currency adopted on cargo ships is usually the US Dollar or the Euro.

Bottle of wine (1l)	$1.15
Pringles Chips	$3.49
Chocolate bars (250 gr)	$4.25
Beer cans (12 can pack)	$17.20
Jack Daniels whiskey (75 cl)	$19.00
Coca-Cola (12 can pack)	$10.70
Six bottles of mineral water	$5.40
Peanuts (150 gr)	$3.20
Deodorant (75 ml)	$5.80
Toothpaste	$2.00
Toothbrush	$1.20
Notepad	$2.70
Set of four pens	$3.90
Cigarettes (6 packet stick)	$14.80

Table 3

Chapter 6

Unexpected circumstances and Emergencies on board

And now, what is going to be of my journey? I've studied close and hard without knowing anything. The unexpected is the only hope. But, they tell me, it is foolish to tell oneself that.

Eugenio Montale

Sea sickness

The weather is a constant concern for the captain. Wind speed and direction, water temperature and salinity, currents, rain and fog, all affect the ship's movement. If this is your first time on a ship, you probably don't know whether you suffer sea sickness or not. Luckily, today there are different remedies available for this problem.

I think I can safely say that unless you are an extremely sensitive person, it's quite difficult to suffer seasickness on a cargo boat. Why? This is why: in general, the bigger the vessel, the lesser you feel its movement. You can compare it with the Earth's rotation around the Sun. The Earth rotates at a speed of 30 kilometres per second, but we don't feel its movement, do we? We don't feel it at all! A cargo ship is very big and doesn't totter at the first wave like a small sailing boat.

Nevertheless, having said this, there are still situations in which you may feel seasickness on a cargo boat, when, for example:

- The sea is extremely rough. In such a situation, it's impossible not to feel the movement, even on the biggest vessels in existence. Don't worry. The captain's expertise will deal with any eventual extreme conditions in the best way possible;

- The ship is not fully loaded. When the ship is lighter, it is more subject to the sea's movements;
- The ship's direction is against the waves' direction. If you are asking yourself what this might mean, I understand: I found it difficult to comprehend until I too experienced it myself. Even when the sea is calm, there are always outside factors that provoke light waves, such as wind and underwater currents. Especially in the open sea. Generally, the captain will try to follow these movements, or at least, not to go against them. In some situations, though, this is not possible. For example, when a cargo ship is about to leave the Mediterranean heading South. If, at that moment, the waves are following a horizontal direction (like, from East to West), the vessel's direction will be perpendicular to the waves' movement. The captain, in this case, can't do much because he must follow his route. But this is the worst-case scenario of a ship subjected to the movement of the waves and in which you'll rock a bit.

To be safe, I suggest you bring one or two packets of medicine for seasickness on board with you. I'm not a doctor, so it would be better to ask your doctor before making any decision about it.

What happens if someone becomes sick?

Unlike cruise ships, cargo boats don't carry a doctor on board. The

Admiralty Law states that the obligation of having a doctor on board is only for ships that carry more than twelve passengers. For this reason, cargo ships have a limited number of passengers, and that's why you must provide a certificate of good health and travel insurance before sailing.

Obviously, it is possible that a member of the crew falls sick. Cargo ships have an infirmary appropriately equipped to deal with minor illnesses and emergencies. Moreover, all officers must take first aid courses.

However, you should be prepared in case you happen to get sick.

In Chapter 2, we pointed out that a medical kit is one of the essentials to pack in your luggage. Even though the infirmary might be equipped with all the medicines you may need, I suggest you bring your own ones. You could be allergic to some medicine without knowing it and finding this out while on board a ship in the middle of the ocean away from civilisation wouldn't be a pleasant experience.

If you do get sick, do exactly what you would at home. If you need to lay down, do so. If you're travelling with someone else, they can bring you some food to your cabin; otherwise, you can ask the steward to bring your meals.

As mentioned before, seek your doctor's advice before leaving or before making any decisions.

What will happen if someone has an accident?

It is possible that someone has an accident on board. If the person's condition is serious, the captain will contact the relevant emergency services via satellite to deal with the situation.

It's important you understand that a cargo ship is not a rundown vessel full of dangers. It's like any other ship. The off-limits areas are well signed.

If you are travelling with children, the same thing applies. Act with them as you would at home. You wouldn't let your small children cross a main road in a city by themselves, would you?

Remember: accidents can happen, no matter what. The ship's infirmary and the crew can help with first aid. If you hurt yourself, call the steward immediately. He'll know what to do.

What happens if the engine breaks down?

This is a more likely scenario than previous ones. Cargo ships sail twenty-four hours a day, seven days a week. In the event, the engine breaks down, the vessel carries a number of spare parts, and the Head Engineer should be able to fix any problem that is not too complicated. If, however, the breakdown is unfixable on the spot, the Captain will have to call a tugboat to drag the ship to the nearest port to be repaired.

Emergency Drills

During the trip, the captain might organise one or more emergency drills. These exercises aim to verify different aspects of safety on board.

For example, fire in the engine room, man overboard, pirate attack, or ship evacuation. My friend told me that on the cargo ship he was travelling on they had an emergency drill to search for a bomb.

Amongst all of these different types of emergency procedures, the most detailed one is for a man overboard. It was thoroughly explained to me by a member of the crew who had experienced this firsthand. If it happens that someone falls into the sea, one of the crewmembers must first throw an orange lifebuoy with a floating light in the water attached. Then the alarm is activated, and the ship's position is automatically marked on the maps by GPS. The head engineer starts to slow the ship down to prepare it for a turning manoeuvre. It must be done slowly; otherwise, there is the risk the vessel might turn upside down. Each member of the crew has his own specific duties during an emergency safety plan. The chef prepares hot drinks and blankets for the person overboard. Another crewmember prepares the infirmary equipment, making sure the oxygen tank is ready. When the ship is close to the victim, a lifeboat is launched into the water to go and recover the person.

It must be a very dreadful experience, falling into the open sea and watching your ship moving rapidly away from you.

Only the crew partakes in the emergency drills, whereas the evacuation exercises involve the passengers as well. If these exercises take place while you are on board, strictly follow the captain's instructions, without being too stiff about it. This is part of your adventure and will only enrich it and give you more insight into life at sea.

Pirates

Despite the fact that we are living in the 21st Century, the problem of piracy still exists. Stories such as the one of Captain Phillips (which was turned into a movie, magnificently starring Tom Hanks) are living proof. Some cargo ships may follow routes that cross pirate-infested waters.

The majority of merchant vessels are not armed. However, in the case that the ship has to go through pirate-infested waters, the captain can hire armed staff to protect it. If there is a threat, the captain has to assess the seriousness of the situation and give permission to the armed escort to act. Their first move will be a warning shot in the air. If the pirates keep coming closer, the escort is authorised to shoot into the water near the approaching pirate ship. As a last measure, the ship or its crew will become the target. Hoses and fire extinguishers will be the principal deterrents against pirates who are trying to come aboard. Some cargo ships will also put barbed wire on those parts of the ship that are vulnerable to attacks, like the poop deck.

Captains, in general, prefer to travel in pirate-infested waters at full speed or during bad weather and rough seas. In these conditions, the small vessels pirates use are forced to remain in the harbour.

Pirates operate principally in South-East Asia and off the east coast of Africa. If you have a trip in Europe or towards the Americas, you won't have to think about this.

Luckily, the frequency of the attacks has considerably diminished during the last years. The International Maritime Bureau (IMB) reported that during the past eight years the number of pirate attacks has decreased to an unprecedented minimum level. The only exception is the Malaysian coast, where in 2014 the attacks went from 12 to 21. Attacks around Somalian waters (where the film about Captain Phillips is set) have been effectively eliminated. The number of cases of piracy in these waters has decreased from 237 in 2011 to 15 in 2014. Success in Somalian waters can be put down to four factors:

- The presence of private armed guards aboard ships;
- The employment of evasive manoeuvres;
- Actions preventing the chance of pirate ships leaving the coast;
- Political change in Somalia, resulting in lower tolerance for pirates.

Google Earth has turned out to be one of the principal instruments for prevention against pirates in Somalia. Information and coordinates were collected from various sources: maritime organisations, governments and insurance companies. The mapping includes high-definition satellite images that identify the actual premises of the pirates.

Chapter 7

Arrival at your destination

Arriving at each new city, the traveller finds again a past of his that he did not know he had: the foreignness of what you no longer are or no longer possess lies in wait for you in foreign, unpossessed places.

Italo Calvino, *Invisible Cities*

A few days before arrival, the captain will contact you to give you instructions for the disembarkation procedure.

The day of your arrival, pack your bags and make sure you haven't left any belongings in the cabin. The captain will tell you to wait for the port taxi, which will take you outside the port area. You'll probably have to wait for an hour or two, so be prepared and keep a book at hand.

This is also the time to say your goodbyes.

In this book I have tried to help you to plan a journey on a cargo ship and told you what to expect on board. To organise and accomplish a trip of this kind may seem difficult, if not impossible, at first, but if you follow the instructions and tips I have given you on this book, you'll realise that it's actually very easy. I hope this guide has inspired you to turn your thoughts into actions. There is a saying in Italian which translates something like this: 'Between what is said and what is done, there is an ocean.' In this case, this "ocean" couldn't be more apt.

Bon voyage!

Acknowledgments

I'd like to thank first of all my family. Barbara, my wife, has been a firm support during the entire creation process of this guidebook. I thank her for her patience in dealing with my 'writer's' moods, like when I woke up at 6:30 a.m. to write. I thank her for her love, which kept me going and stopped me from giving up even when it seemed there was no time at all for me to write.

I thank my parents, who bear with love and understanding my whereabouts and adventures around the world.

A special thanks goes to all the crewmembers of the MSC Geneva, who made my journey on that ship unforgettable (it wasn't taken for granted that it would be). To Quarry, for his astronomy lessons, improvised on the deck. To Marika, for having shared with me her experience as the only female member of the crew. To Gunda, who showed me (just a glimpse!) his secret book of recipes. To Roman's friendship, and with whom I shared the best tapas of my life in Valencia. To Jens, for all the stories with which he accompanied my journey on a cargo ship. To all the Filipino crew, who taught me that it takes little to feel happy in life. To Thomas and Andrea, to their children Lukas e Felix, the best company a person can have on a trip like this.

Thanks also go to Valentina Rossini and Gabriel Rowland for the English translation. To Stuart and Ciaran, who helped me with the proofreading and to all the other people who have read the manuscript. To those who believed in it and encouraged it. To Chandler, who helped me to overcome blank sheet syndrome. To Piernicola, who taught me to do in one day what I would never have thought I would be able to do in three days. To those who read the manuscript a million times. To whoever was there for me, even when it was impossible for them to be.

Thank you.

Author's notes

Federico Lepri is a traveller, writer and blogger. He loves experimentation in his existence, which changes in slow motion, day by day. In 2008 he took the French route of the Camino de Santiago de Compostela and walked over 800 Km.
Four years later he made his first voyage on a freighter ship from Barcelona (Spain) to Santos (Brazil). In 2013 he continued his travels through South America on a 50cc motorbike. He lived for three years in Chile, and he defines himself a citizen of the world.
He currently lives in London, where he is working on a new book and planning his next adventure.

Thank you again for your reading. If you would like, you can also read my diary of the journey I made from Spain to Brazil at the following link:
www.federicolepri.com

At the same link you can also find the book resources.

Bibliography

Bob Hartley, *Around the World by Freighter.* Trafford Publishing, 2004. Print.

Robert D. Rieffel, *Twenty-Eight Days on a Freighter: A Guide for Those with an Interest in Freighter Voyages.* Robert D. Rieffel, 2013. Print.

Piernicola De Maria, *Efficacia personale* [Personal effectiveness]. Libreria Strategica, 2014. Print.

David Allen, *Getting Things Done: The Art of Stress-Free Productivity.* Piatkus, 2002. Print.

Maris Freighter Cruises, *Seaworthy News.* Online publication, 2015.

Table of Contents

Made in the USA
San Bernardino, CA
13 May 2017